UNBELIEVABLE!

34 AMAZING FACTS ABOUT GHOSTS

Tracy Sue Walker

Lerner Publications ◆ Minneapolis

For Wendy Miervaldis—Boo!

Lerner Publications Company
An imprint of Lerner Publishing Group, Inc.
241 First Avenue North
Minneapolis, MN 55401 USA

For reading levels and more information, look up this title at www.lernerbooks.com.

Main body text set in ITC Franklin Gothic Std.
Typeface provided by Adobe Systems.

Editor: Angel Kidd **Designer:** Mary Ross **Photo Editor:** Elena Mai
Lerner team: Martha Kranes

Library of Congress Cataloging-in-Publication Data

Names: Walker, Tracy Sue author
Title: 34 amazing facts about ghosts / Tracy Sue Walker.
Other titles: Thirty four amazing facts about ghosts
Description: Minneapolis : Lerner Publications, [2026] | Series: Unbelievable! (updog books) | Includes bibliographical references and index. | Audience: Ages 8–11 | Audience: Grades 2–3 | Summary: "Ghost hunters use thermal cameras and other cool tech to search for spirits such as poltergeists. Readers uncover more fun facts about haunted locations and famous ghosts in this spooky book"—Provided by publisher.
Identifiers: LCCN 2025013204 (print) | LCCN 2025013205 (ebook) | ISBN 9798765689738 library binding | ISBN 9798348029494 paperback | ISBN 9798765699584 epub
Subjects: LCSH: Ghosts—Juvenile literature
Classification: LCC BF1461 .W346 2026 (print) | LCC BF1461 (ebook) | DDC 133.1—dc23/eng/20250611

LC record available at https://lccn.loc.gov/2025013204
LC ebook record available at https://lccn.loc.gov/2025013205

Manufactured in the United States of America
1-1012512-54841-6/23/2025

Table of Contents

MANY KINDS OF GHOSTS

Many people believe in ghosts. Many don't. There is no scientific proof they exist.

Believers think ghosts are spirits of people who have died.

Some ghosts still look like people, but you can see through them.

Other ghosts look like fog or mist. Some look like floating balls or orbs.

Sometimes ghosts can make noises. They may knock or moan.

There are different kinds of ghosts. Poltergeists are ghosts that like to play tricks.

Up Next!

SOMETHING SPOOKY.

HAUNTED PLACES

Haunted places have ghosts. Some houses or cemeteries are haunted.

Places of pain and anger, such as battlefields, often have ghosts.

The Gettysburg Battlefield is one of the most haunted places in the world.

The Queen Mary is a famous haunted ship.

The Winchester Mystery House is one of the most haunted houses in the world.

Some people think the White House in Washington, DC, is haunted.

LIST BREAK!

What are the top five most haunted cities in the United States?

1. New Orleans, Louisiana
2. Chicago, Illinois
3. Savannah, Georgia
4. Saint Augustine, Florida
5. Portland, Oregon

New Orleans, Louisiana

Slimer

Here are five famous ghosts from books and movies!

1. Slimer from *Ghostbusters*
2. Zero from *The Nightmare Before Christmas*
3. The hitchhiker ghost from European folklore
4. The Ghost of Christmas Past from *A Christmas Carol*
5. Casper the Friendly Ghost from TV and movies

Up Next!

GHOST STARS.

FAMOUS GHOSTS

Many people who visit the White House think it is haunted by Abraham Lincoln.

People think his ghost is in the Lincoln Bedroom.

The Bell Witch is another famous ghost. It haunted a farm in Tennessee in the 1800s.

This ghost shook the house and made spooky noises, scaring the family inside.

Bloody Mary is a famous ghost that is also a game.

If you say Bloody Mary three times in front of a mirror, she may appear.

Up Next!

ARE THEY REAL?

HUNTING FOR GHOSTS

People have been trying to talk to ghosts for thousands of years.

Ghost hunters look for ghosts in places people think are haunted.

Ghost hunters search with technology such as thermal cameras.

Thermal camera

Video recorders and Electronic Voice Phenomena recorders are other useful tools.

Researching the history of a haunted site is important to ghost hunters.

Whether you believe in them or not, ghosts are always an interesting topic.

Some jails may be haunted.

Glossary

battlefield: a place where a battle or fighting has taken place

Electronic Voice Phenomena recorder: a machine used to capture unexplained or unclear voices

folklore: stories that are handed down through generations

orb: a round globe of light

thermal camera: a camera that uses heat to create images

Check It Out!

Britannica Kids: Ghost
https://kids.britannica.com/kids/article/ghost/574605

Carlson-Berne, Emma. *Ghost Hunters*. Lerner Publications, 2024.

Katz, Susan B. *Famous Ghosts*. Lerner Publications, 2024.

Kiddle: Ghost Facts for Kids
https://kids.kiddle.co/Ghost

National Geographic Kids: Haunted Castles
https://www.natgeokids.com/wp-content/uploads/2017/04/Haunted-Castles.pdf

Olson, Gillia M. *Curious about Haunted Places*. Amicus, 2022.

Index

Photo Acknowledgments

Image credits: Cavan Images/Getty Images, pp. 3, 23; David Wall/Getty Images, pp. 4, 25; JohnGollop/Getty Images, p. 5; urbazon/Getty Images, p. 6; Westend61/Getty Images, p. 7; KinoMasterskaya/Shutterstock, pp. 8, 27; THEPALMER/Getty Images, p. 9; Thomas_Zsebok_Images/Getty Images, p. 10; Zeferli/Getty Images, p. 11; AmyDreves/Getty Images, p. 12; Neil Rabinowitz/Getty Images, p. 13; Orange Grove/Shutterstock, p. 14; Waqas_creatives/Shutterstock, p. 15; Edwin Remsberg/Getty Images, p. 16; Mike Marsland/WireImage/Getty Images, p. 17; FPG/Getty Images, p. 18; Gibson Moss/Alamy, p. 19; Maskot/Getty Images, pp. 20, 24; shaunl/Getty Images, p. 21; Renphoto/Getty Images, p. 22; ivansmuk/Getty Images, p. 26; Rebecca Harding/Getty Images, p. 28; Terryfic3D/Getty Images, p. 29.

Cover: David Wall/Getty Images.